Learning to BUDGET

AGS

by
Larry M. Parsky, Ph.D.

AGS®

American Guidance Service, Inc.
4201 Woodland Road
Circle Pines, MN 55014-1796
1-800-328-2560

Printed in the United States of America

ISBN 0–7854–0953–X (Previously ISBN 0–86601–674–0)

Product Number 90861

A 0 9 8 7 6 5

Contents

Unit 6: Budgets and Cash Records

Developing Money Management Skills Lesson 1

Introduction

Developing good money management skills is important. Read the terms listed in the box below. Understanding these terms is the first step in becoming a good money manager.

Terms to Know	
Money manager	a person who handles his or her money wisely
Money management	a plan for spending money wisely
Inflation	an increase in the amount of money in circulation. This increase causes a drop in value and a rise in prices. A product costs more money this year than it did last year.
Budget	a plan for spending a person's income
Estimated income	the amount of money that a person expects to receive during the budget period
Estimated expenses	the items that a person plans to buy with his or her income
Budget record form	a form used to record a person's estimated income and estimated expenses

People complain that their money buys less this year than last year. Food, housing, clothes, and cars cost more money each year. This is caused by inflation. *Inflation* means that the value of products has dropped and that prices have risen. It takes more money to buy an item that once cost less money. An example is a 60¢ candy bar that once cost 40¢. Another example is a $100.00 raincoat that once cost $75.00. Inflation makes it difficult for people to buy the basic things they need. Can you think of other examples of inflation? What can people do about inflation? It seems that everyone must use better money management skills.

U
N
I
T

1

This book will teach you the money management skill of preparing a budget. You will understand why it is important to have a budget plan and how to prepare a budget that will chart your income and expenses.

A *budget* is a plan to show how a person plans to spend his or her income for a certain period of time. A person has to consider two things when planning a budget: estimated income and estimated expenses.

Estimated income is the amount of money a person expects to receive in a certain period of time. This income is usually the person's earnings (salary or wages). Earnings are the amount of money a person receives for work done. *Gross earnings* are the total amount of money earned before any deductions are taken. A budget must be planned around the *net earnings*, or the actual cash a person has to spend after deductions are taken out.

Estimated expenses are the items (products, services, or activities) a person plans to buy with estimated income. Estimated expenses cannot be more than the estimated income. You cannot buy what you do not have money for!

A budget plan must cover a certain period of time. It can be prepared for the days within a pay period or for one month at a time. A pay period is not the same for all workers. Some workers are paid once a week; others are paid once every two weeks. Some workers are paid once a month. In this book, the budgets will be prepared for a two-week period or for a one-month period. The following case history will show you how to plan a budget.

Case History: Joey Mandez
Joey Mandez works as a lab technician at the Fairview Medical Center. Joey did not always use good money management skills. He did not manage his money well. He was always broke. He could not pay his bills or save money for vacations or extras. Often he borrowed money from his father. Joey wanted to be a good money manager. His parents finally suggested that he prepare a budget to help him manage his money better.

At first, Joey did not think that a budget plan would work. He thought that a pay raise would solve his money problems. His parents said that he must learn to live on his present income.

Joey was disappointed when he prepared his first budget. The budget showed that he still could not pay for all of the things that he wanted. Remember that his expenses must cover ten working days and whatever activities he wants to do on two weekends. Look at Joey's budget below.

Budget Record Form

Joey Mandez
For Pay Period March 1 to March 15, 1998

Cash on Hand:	8	76
Estimated Income (Salary/Wages):	285	87
TOTAL ESTIMATED CASH:	294	63
Estimated Expenses:		
New Clothes	50	00
Entertainment	30	00
Vacation Fund	30	00
Lunches	50	00
Gifts	20	00
Bus Fare	20	00
Room & Board	50	00
Payment for Dental Exam	70	00
Miscellaneous Expenses	20	00

TOTAL ESTIMATED EXPENSES $	340	00

Total Estimated Cash $	294	63
Total Estimated Expenses —	340	00
CASH ON HAND (end of Budget Period)	— 45	37

Balancing a Budget

UNIT 1

What is wrong with Joey's budget? It does not balance. His expenses are greater than his income. A person cannot spend more money than he or she earns. A person must live within his or her budget. This means that a person's expenses cannot be more than his or her income.

What can Joey do to balance his budget? He can increase his income. This is unlikely since he just got a raise. His estimated expenses *must* be lower than his income.

What suggestions would you make for balancing Joey's budget? Use the budget record form on the next page. Help Joey prepare a balanced budget.

Consider these points:

1. Does Joey list his most important expenses first?

2. Look at his estimated money for lunch expenses. Could he cut down on these expenses?

3. Look at his estimated money for gifts. Is this a need or a want?

4. Look at his estimated money for new clothes. Should Joey reduce this amount?

5. Look at his estimated money for miscellaneous expenses. Can Joey afford $20.00 each pay period for odds and ends?

Use the budget record form below. Rewrite Joey's budget, which was shown on page 7. Change the figures that he estimated for each expense. Remember that the total of his estimated expenses cannot be more than the total of his estimated income: $294.63. If he spends less than this amount, he will have cash on hand at the end of the budget period.

Budget Record Form

Cash on Hand:

Estimated Income (Salary/Wages):

TOTAL ESTIMATED CASH:

Estimated Expenses:

TOTAL ESTIMATED EXPENSES $

Total Estimated Cash $

Total Estimated Expenses —

CASH ON HAND
(end of Budget Period)

Review Unit 1

A Read the following list of terms carefully. Choose the correct answer for each sentence. Write your answers on the lines provided.

- inflation
- budget
- estimated expenses
- money manager
- money management
- estimated income
- budget record form
- gross earnings

1. A _____ is a plan to show how a person will spend his or her income.

2. _____ can cause an item to cost more money today than it did last year.

3. A _____ is a person who handles his or her money wisely.

4. A person uses a _____ to see whether the budget plan is being followed.

5. _____ is the amount of money a person expects to earn.

6. Being able to prepare a budget is an important _____ skill to have.

7. _____ are items that a person plans to buy with his or her income.

8. The total amount of money earned in a pay period is called _____ .

B Match the definitions in Column 2 with the correct terms in Column 1.

Column 1

_____ 9. A budget record form
_____ 10. Estimated income
_____ 11. A money manager
_____ 12. Inflation
_____ 13. Estimated expenses
_____ 14. A budget
_____ 15. Money management
_____ 16. Net earnings

Column 2

a. is a plan for spending money.

b. can cause items to cost more money today than they did last year.

c. is the money you have after deductions are taken from gross earnings.

d. is a person who handles his or her money well.

e. are items that a person plans to buy with his or her income.

f. means spending money wisely.

g. is the money that a person expects to earn.

h. is used to record a budget.

C Define each of the following money management terms.

17. Inflation _____

_____

18. Money management _____

_____

19. Money manager _____

_____

20. Budget _____

_____

21. Estimated income _____

_____

22. Estimated expenses _____

_____

23. Budget record form _____

_____

24. Net earnings _____

_____

Planning a Budget

UNIT 2

Needs, wants, habits, and goals

Several items must be considered before one begins to plan a budget. Read the terms listed in the box below. Understanding these terms will help you plan your budget.

Terms to Know	
Needs	items that a person must have to live
Wants	items that a person would like to have but can live without
Values	the way a person feels about things; a standard that makes things desirable or important
Budget	a plan for spending income during the budget period
Spending habits	the ways a person tends to spend money
Goals	an object or end that one works to accomplish; goals help a person plan how to get important things
Gross income	the total amount of money that a person earns
Net income	the amount of money a person takes home after deductions (for example, taxes) have been taken out

Spending habits

Preparing a budget is not an easy task. You may have to change your spending habits if you spend money freely. Your spending habits determine whether you spend money on things you need or on things you want. *Needs* and *wants* are terms that will be used to describe the kinds of items a person buys with income. Joey's mother and father had a long talk with Joey about how he should examine his needs and wants as he plans his budget.

Needs and wants

Joey discovered that he had many bad spending habits. He wanted to change these habits. To help him manage his money better, he needed to revise his budget. The first step was to make a list of his needs and wants.

Needs are basic things that people must have. These include food, clothing, housing, and medical care. *Wants* are things that people like but that are not essential to their survival. Such wants can include buying a new stereo, having an expensive television, radio, or camera, or taking a vacation.

Look at Joey's list of needs and wants below. Do you agree with the items on his list? Would you make any changes? Explain your reasons.

Needs	**Wants**
1. Room and board	1. New clothes
2. Bus fare to and from work	2. Entertainment
3. Medical expenses	3. Vacation
4. Grooming aids	4. New stereo
5. Lunches	5. New watch
6. Savings	6. Taking golf lessons
7. Health and life insurance	7. Set of golf clubs
	8. Gifts for birthdays and Christmas
	9. Used car

Setting goals for a budget

Joey has many needs and wants on his list. He cannot afford to buy all the items on the two lists with his income. He must reduce the number of items on his lists. He must make important decisions. If he buys one item, he may not buy another item.

The items on his needs list are basic to his survival. For example, money for bus fare and lunches makes it possible for him to work. Can you explain why other items on his needs list are basic to his survival? The items on his wants list are things that he can live without. Joey must make changes in this list. He must make decisions.

What Do You Want to Spend Your Money On?

Improving a Budget

To improve his budget, Joey must make decisions about his wants and needs. He decided to look at his needs first. He would make a decision about each one.

Needs	Decisions
1. Savings	He did not save money before he prepared a budget. He now plans to save $30.00 each pay period.
2. Room and board	Joey lives at home with his parents. Paying only $50.00 for room and board is a big savings for him. If he lived in an apartment on his own, he would pay much more. He would also have to pay for meals.
3. Bus fare, lunches, miscellaneous expenses	Joey cut back in these three areas so that his budget will balance this pay period. In his next pay period, he will have more money to spend on these items.

Joey then reviewed the items on his wants list. He made the following changes:

Wants	Decisions
1. New clothes	He will not buy any new clothes now. He plans to wait for summer and winter sales in department stores.
2. Entertainment	He will spend less money. He will spend $20 instead of $30.
3. Vacation	He was saving $30.00 each pay period. He will take a less expensive vacation next summer. He will now save $20 each pay period instead of $30.
4. New stereo	He will delay this purchase. He does not have enough money. He will save $5.00 each pay period until he has enough money to buy the stereo. How long do you think it will take to save enough money?
5. New watch	His present watch works well. He will not buy a new watch.
6. Other items	Each pay period he will try to save money in order to buy these items at a future date.

Let us look at Joey's new budget for this next pay period. You will find a copy of his new budget on page 15. Joey made decisions about his lists of needs and wants. Do you agree with the changes he made? His new budget now balances. He also made up the $45.37 that he was short in his last budget.

Budget Record Form

Joey Mandez
For Pay Period March 16 to March 31, 1998

Cash on Hand:	—45	37
Estimated Income (Salary/Wages):	285	87
TOTAL ESTIMATED CASH:	240	50
Estimated Expenses:		
Room and Board	50	00
Lunches	30	00
Bus Fare	25	00
Savings	30	00
Vacation Fund	20	00
Medical Expenses	15	00
Entertainment	20	00
Stereo Fund	5	00
Grooming Needs	20	00
Clothing Fund	20	00
Miscellaneous Expenses	5	50
TOTAL ESTIMATED EXPENSES	$ 240	50

Total Estimated Cash	$ 240	50
Total Estimated Expenses —	240	50
CASH ON HAND (end of Budget Period)	0	00

Deciding personal habits

Joey has been thinking about his personal values. He used his list of wants and needs to set goals for himself. Setting goals will help him make better decisions about spending his income. Goals will help him prepare a budget that should leave him with some cash on hand at the end of the budget period.

Here are two of the goals that Joey set to help him manage his money better.

1. Provide for his needs first.

2. Any money left over will be used to obtain some of his wants.

Everyone makes decisions about what they consider to be important. Joey decided that he did not need a new watch. He decided that it was important to save some money each pay period. However, all people do not value the same things. Someone else may have decided that a new watch was more important than a new stereo. Do you agree with Joey's goals for spending his income? Do you agree with how he cut back on his wants list? There are no right or wrong answers. You may have good reasons for where you think the money should be spent. Your reasons are influenced by your values.

Values suggest how people feel about things. Such values determine what a person thinks is important. People learn their values when they are young. Values influence people's decisions.

There is nothing wrong with people having different values. It is only important that people be responsible for their decisions. One person's decisions should not interfere with other people's rights. If the decision that you make affects other people, then you must consider their rights and needs as well as your own wants.

Spending habits

Your spending habits require you to make decisions. Decision-making skills help you decide where you can best spend the money that you have. You must consider all the possible choices for spending your money. You should think carefully about each choice. Then you can decide which one is the best. Discussing the choices with another person is a good idea. This person could be a parent or a good friend.

Your choices and spending habits are affected by the needs and wants that you have. This is true for all people. Some people do not always manage their money well. They spend more money than they earn. They often go into debt. They have poor spending habits.

What can people do to solve their money problems? The first thing that they will have to do is change their spending habits. Making a list of their needs and wants is helpful. Then they should ask themselves the following questions:

1. Which items must I have in order to live?

2. Which items do I like but can live without?

3. Which items should I do without until I solve my money problems?

The following pages contain case histories and activities about people with money problems. These people have poor spending habits. You will evaluate their needs and wants. You will make decisions about how they should spend their money. You will help them change their spending habits.

Changing Spending Habits

A Two-Week Plan

A Joey is ready to prepare his budget for the next two weeks. Help him write his budget plan for the pay period of June 1 to June 15. Write his figures on the budget record form on page 19.

1. Joey will have the following income. List them on the budget record form.
   Cash on hand—$12.10
   Salary—$285.87

2. Write the total of Joey's estimated cash on the form.

3. Joey estimates several expenses. List them on the budget record form.
   Savings—$25.00
   Room and Board—$50.00
   Lunches—$40.00
   Bus Fare—$40.00
   Vacation Fund—$20.00
   Medical Expenses—$25.00
   Entertainment—$20.00
   Gift Fund—$9.50
   Grooming Needs—$10.00
   Clothing Fund—$20.00
   Miscellaneous Expenses—$25.00

4. Write the total of Joey's estimated expenses on the form.

B Answer the following questions about Joey Mandez's budget.

5. How much is Joey's estimated income? _____

6. How much are Joey's estimated expenses? _____

7. The money left over at the end of a budget period is called *cash on hand.* To get this figure, subtract the total estimated expenses from the total estimated cash. How much money does Joey expect to have at the end of his two-week budget period? _____

8. Write this cash-on-hand figure on your budget record form.

Budget Record Form

Cash on Hand:

Estimated Income (Salary/Wages):

TOTAL ESTIMATED CASH:

Estimated Expenses:

TOTAL ESTIMATED EXPENSES $

Total Estimated Cash $

Total Estimated Expenses —

CASH ON HAND
(end of Budget Period)

In the last lesson, you looked at the budget of a single person. Now you are going to consider the needs and wants of a married couple. You will see how these needs and wants affect their budget. Bill and Laura Clark are poor money managers. They always have trouble paying their bills. They are often broke. A credit counselor suggested that they look at their spending habits. She asked them to make a list of their needs and wants. Here is their list.

Needs	Wants
1. Money for a down payment on a house	1. Entertainment
2. Food	2. New television set
3. Rent payment	3. New sofa
4. Two store charge account payments	4. New car
5. Car payment	5. New kitchen appliances
6. Two credit card payments	6. Vacation

Evaluate the Clarks' spending habits.

1. Write a sentence about the Clarks' spending habits.

_____

_____

2. How many payments do the Clarks have to make?

_____

_____

3. List three reasons why the Clarks are having problems managing their money.

_____

_____

_____

4. List the changes that the Clarks should make in their spending habits.

_____

_____

_____

5. Bill Clark has take-home pay of $875.28. He does not have any cash on hand this month. Prepare a budget that will pay some money on all of the Clarks' bills. Decide how much will be paid for each item on the Clarks' list. Use the form on this page. The total expenses must not be more than Bill's take-home pay.

Budget Record Form

Cash on Hand:

Estimated Income (Salary/Wages):

TOTAL ESTIMATED CASH:

Estimated Expenses:

TOTAL ESTIMATED EXPENSES $

Total Estimated Cash $

Total Estimated Expenses —

CASH ON HAND
(end of Budget Period)

Evaluating Needs and Wants: Case 2

You are now going to evaluate the needs and wants of another single person. Rick Argenta works as an auto mechanic at Wingate Automotive Center. He owes his creditors money. He has a bad credit rating. His employer suggested that he look at his spending habits. He told Rick to make a list of his needs and wants. Here is Rick's list.

Needs	Wants
1. Rent payment	1. Groceries
2. New motorcycle	2. Medical bills
3. New leather coat	3. Stereo for car
4. Entertainment	4. Credit card payment
5. Utility bill payment	5. Concert ticket

Evalulate Rick's spending habits.

1. Rick did not put all of his needs and wants in the correct columns. List the changes that you would make in each list.

Needs	Wants
a. _____	f. _____
b. _____	g. _____
c. _____	h. _____
d. _____	i. _____
e. _____	j. _____

2. Write a sentence about Rick's spending habits.

_____

_____

3. List three reasons why Rick is having problems managing his money.

_____

_____

_____

4. List the changes that Rick should make in his spending habits.

_____

_____

5. Rick's take-home pay is $596.32. He has no cash on hand. Prepare a monthly budget for him that will cover all of his needs and some of his wants. Do not go by Rick's list. You will need to decide what his important needs and wants should be. Use the budget record form on this page. Remember that Rick's total expenses must not be more than his take-home pay.

Budget Record Form

Cash on Hand:

Estimated Income (Salary/Wages):

TOTAL ESTIMATED CASH:

Estimated Expenses:

TOTAL ESTIMATED EXPENSES $

Total Estimated Cash $

Total Estimated Expenses —

CASH ON HAND
(end of Budget Period)

Evaluating Needs and Wants: Case 3

UNIT 2

Lesson 5

Marie and Tony Santos have money problems. They have trouble paying their bills. They borrowed money from their credit union. Tony's boss suggested that they look at their spending habits. He told them to make a list of their needs and wants. Here is Marie and Tony's list.

Needs	Wants
1. New television	1. Medical bills
2. Rent payment	2. Payment of charge account
3. Payment of phone bill	3. New sofa
4. Tickets for concert	4. Groceries
5. New kitchen appliances	5. New car

Are These Items Examples of Needs or Wants?

■ Evaluate Marie and Tony's spending habits.

1. Marie and Tony have some of their needs and wants listed in the wrong columns. Write the changes that you would make in each list.

Needs	Wants
a. _____	f. _____
b. _____	g. _____
c. _____	h. _____
d. _____	i. _____
e. _____	j. _____

2. Write a sentence about Tony and Marie's spending habits.

_____

_____

_____

3. List three reasons why Marie and Tony are having problems managing their money.

_____

_____

_____

_____

_____

4. List the changes that Tony and Marie should make in their spending habits.

_____

_____

_____

_____

_____

_____

_____

Evaluating Needs and Wants: Case 4

Dave and Lois Dulansey are a couple with two teenagers. They cannot pay their bills. They cannot seem to get out of debt. A credit counselor asked them to look at their spending habits. She told them to make a list of their needs and wants. Here is their list.

Needs	**Wants**
1. Food	1. Doctors' bills
2. New television set	2. Money owed to friends
3. Mortgage payment	3. Living room furniture
4. Washing machine	4. Credit card payment
5. Utility bills	5. Video camera payment
6. Tickets for concert	6. A third car
7. Two car payments	

■ Read Lois and Dave's needs and wants list above. Then evaluate their spending habits.

1. Do you agree with the items on Lois and Dave's needs and wants list? _____

2. If you do not agree, write the changes that you would make in the list. Write your answers on the lines below. There is not an even number of wants and needs in their list. You will not need to write on all of the lines.

Needs	**Wants**
a. _____	i. _____
b. _____	j. _____
c. _____	k. _____
d. _____	l. _____
e. _____	m. _____
f. _____	n. _____
g. _____	o. _____
h. _____	p. _____

3. Write a sentence about Lois and Dave's spending habits.

_____

_____

4. List three reasons why Lois and Dave are having problems managing their money.

_____

_____

_____

5. List the changes that Dave and Lois should make in their spending habits.

_____

_____

_____

6. Dave and Lois both work. Their take-home pay each month is $3,285.76. Prepare a budget for them that will pay some money on all of their needs items. Use the needs and wants list you made for them on the previous page. Remember that they have two children and no cash on hand. Use the budget record form on page 28.

How Can Dave and Lois Budget Money for New Furniture?

Budget Record Form

_____

_____

_____

Cash on Hand:

Estimated Income (Salary/Wages):

TOTAL ESTIMATED CASH:

Estimated Expenses:

TOTAL ESTIMATED EXPENSES $

Total Estimated Cash $ _____

Total Estimated Expenses — _____

CASH ON HAND
(end of Budget Period)

Evaluating Your Needs and Wants

This activity will help you learn more about your spending habits. Your spending habits include your needs and wants. Remember that *needs* are things that you must have. *Wants* are things that you can do without. Pretend that you are a single person. You are working at your first job. You have take-home pay of $400.00 each week. You are going to plan your budget for a one-week period.

A Make a list of your five most important needs and wants. List your most important needs and wants first.

Needs	Wants
1. _____	1. _____
2. _____	2. _____
3. _____	3. _____
4. _____	4. _____
5. _____	5. _____

B Read the following statements. Respond to each statement.

6. Look at your list. Are all needs and wants listed in the correct columns? _____

7. List the wants that you could give up.

_____

_____

_____

_____

8. Write a sentence about your spending habits.

_____

_____

9. Write one good thing about your spending habits.

_____

_____

10. Write one thing that you would like to change about your spending habits.

_____

_____

C Prepare a budget for a one-week period. Decide how much you can spend on all of your needs and at least some of your wants. Remember that your total expenses cannot be more than your take-home pay of $400.00. Use the budget record form below.

Budget Record Form

_____

_____

_____

Cash on Hand:

Estimated Income (Salary/Wages):

TOTAL ESTIMATED CASH:

Estimated Expenses:

_____

_____

_____

_____

_____

_____

_____

_____

_____

_____

_____

_____

_____

TOTAL ESTIMATED EXPENSES $ _____

Total Estimated Cash $ _____

Total Estimated Expenses — _____

CASH ON HAND
(end of Budget Period) _____

Review Unit 2

A Read the following list of terms carefully. Choose the correct answer for each sentence. Write your answers on the lines.

- decision making
- net income
- spending habits
- wants
- goals
- needs
- values

1. _____ are items that a person must have to survive.

2. _____ are how a person uses money.

3. A _____ is a person's take-home pay.

4. _____ includes thinking about how to spend money.

5. _____ are the way that a person feels about things.

6. _____ help a person plan how to get the things he or she wants in life.

7. _____ are items that a person would like to have but can live without.

B Match the definitions in Column 2 with the correct terms in Column 1.

Column 1	Column 2
_____ 8. Goals	a. are items that a person can live without.
_____ 9. A budget	b. show how a person feels about things.
_____ 10. Spending habits	c. involves thinking about how to spend money.
_____ 11. Needs	d. is a plan for spending income.
_____ 12. Values	e. show how a person buys items.
_____ 13. Wants	f. help a person plan to get important items.
_____ 14. Decision making	g. are things that a person must have to live.

C Give one example of each of the following.

15. Goal _____

16. Value _____

17. Decision making _____

18. Need _____

Test Units 1–2

A Choose the correct term to complete each sentence.

inflation   gross   money manager   net

values   budget   needs

1. A good _____ creates a _____ to help keep track of expenses.

2. _____ may make your estimated expenses more than they were last year.

3. Your _____ are essential items that must be included in your budget.

4. Education, family, and hard work are examples of _____.

5. Your _____ income is determined before taxes and other deductions.

6. Your _____ income is what is available after taxes and other deductions.

B Martha Cole is a graduate student who works part-time as a waitress. She needs to revise her spending habits. Organize her expenses into wants and needs. Circle "W" or "N."

7. rent payment   W   or   N

11. groceries   W   or   N

8. new car   W   or   N

12. school books   W   or   N

9. school loans   W   or   N

13. credit card bills   W   or   N

10. utility bill payment   W   or   N

14. new clothes   W   or   N

C Jamal Weaver manages a gas station. Help him prepare his budget for the next two weeks. His cash on hand is $15.35. His salary for the two-week period is $436.82. His expenses are as follows:

Entertainment $26.00   Bus fare $20.00   Rent $137.00   Vacation fund $18.00

Medical expenses $12.00   Savings $30.00   Lunches $31.00   Grooming $14.00

Miscellaneous $6.00   Clothing $53.00   Credit card payments $78.00

15. Make and fill out a budget record form like the one on page 28.

    a. What is Jamal's estimated income? _____

    b. What are Jamal's estimated expenses? _____

    c. What is Jamal's cash on hand at the end of the budget period?

    _____

Case 1

A Help Joey Mandez prepare his budget plan for the pay period of June 16 to June 30. Use the budget record form on page 34.

1. Joey will have the following income. Write these figures on your form.

   Cash on Hand—$14.92

   Salary—$295.57

2. Joey expects the following expenses. Write them on your form.

   Savings—$25.00

   Room and Board—$50.00

   Lunches—$40.00

   Bus Fare—$40.00

   Vacation Fund—$20.00

   Gift Fund—$9.50

   Eye Exam—$35.00

   Grooming Needs—$15.00

   Clothing Fund—$30.00

   Contributions—$15.00

   Miscellaneous Expenses—$25.00

B Answer the following questions about Joey Mandez's budget.

3. How much is Joey's estimated income? _____

4. How much are Joey's estimated expenses? _____

5. How much cash on hand does Joey expect to have at the end of the budget period?

   _____

Budget Record Form

_____
_____
_____

Cash on Hand:
Estimated Income (Salary/Wages):
TOTAL ESTIMATED CASH:

Estimated Expenses:

TOTAL ESTIMATED EXPENSES $

Total Estimated Cash $ _____
Total Estimated Expenses — _____
CASH ON HAND
(end of Budget Period)

Case 2

A Help Joey Mandez prepare his second budget. This budget plan will be for the pay period of July 1 to July 14. Use the budget record form on page 36.

1. Joey will have the following income. Write these figures on the form.

    Cash on Hand—$16.13

    Salary—$295.87

2. Joey expects the following expenses. Write them on the form.

    Savings—$25.00

    Room and Board—$50.00

    Lunches—$40.00

    Vacation Fund—$20.00

    Gift Fund—$9.50

    Dental Exam—$40.00

    Grooming Needs—$10.00

    Clothing Fund—$35.00

    Doctor Bill—$15.00

    Miscellaneous Expenses—$25.00

B Write the answers to the following questions about Joey Mandez's budget.

3. How much is Joey's estimated income? _____

4. How much are Joey's estimated expenses? _____

5. Did Joey live within his budget? _____

6. How much money does Joey expect to have at the end of the budget period?

    _____

7. What is the name given to this money that is left over at the end of a budget period?

    _____

8. Where does this money appear on a budget record form for the next budget period?

    _____

Budget Record Form

_____

_____

_____

Cash on Hand:

Estimated Income (Salary/Wages):

TOTAL ESTIMATED CASH:

Estimated Expenses:

TOTAL ESTIMATED EXPENSES $

Total Estimated Cash $ _____

Total Estimated Expenses — _____

CASH ON HAND
(end of Budget Period)

Case 3

Sam Yancy has money problems. He cannot get credit. His friend Gil suggested that Sam study his spending habits. Gil told him to make a list of his needs and wants. Here is Sam's list.

Needs	Wants
1. Car payment	1. Rent
2. New motorcycle	2. Credit card payment
3. Groceries	3. New CD player
4. Vacation	4. Car repair bill
5. Motorcycle repair	5. Payment for eye exam

Evaluate Sam's list.

1. Are Sam's needs and wants listed in the correct columns? _____

If the needs and wants are not correct, list the changes that you would make in each column. There are not equal numbers of needs and wants. You will not need to use all of the lines below.

Needs	Wants
a. _____	h. _____
b. _____	i. _____
c. _____	j. _____
d. _____	k. _____
e. _____	l. _____
f. _____	m. _____
g. _____	n. _____

2. Write a sentence about Sam's spending habits.

_____

_____

3. List three reasons why Sam is having problems managing his money.

_____

_____

_____

4. List the changes that Sam should make in his spending habits.

_____

_____

5. Sam has $25.00 cash on hand and take-home pay of $472.00 every two weeks. Decide how much he will pay on all of his wants and needs for a two-week period. Fill in his budget record form below. Remember that his expenses cannot be more than his total estimated cash.

Budget Record Form

Cash on Hand:

Estimated Income (Salary/Wages):

TOTAL ESTIMATED CASH:

Estimated Expenses:

TOTAL ESTIMATED EXPENSES $

Total Estimated Cash $

Total Estimated Expenses −

CASH ON HAND
(end of Budget Period)

Case 4

Rita Torres works as a salesperson at Teller's Department Store. She is having trouble paying her bills. Her friend suggested that she study her spending habits. He told her to make a list of her needs and wants. Here is Rita's list.

Needs	Wants
1. New party dress	1. Room and board
2. Car repair bill	2. Tickets for a play
3. Lunches at work	3. Bus fare for work
4. New ring	4. Dentist bill
5. Money for beauty shop	5. Payment on loan from her mother

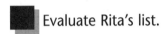 Evaluate Rita's list.

1. List the changes that you would make in Rita's list of needs and wants. There may not be an even number of needs and wants. You will not need to use all of the lines

Needs	Wants
a. _____	f. _____
b. _____	g. _____
c. _____	h. _____
d. _____	i. _____
e. _____	j. _____

2. Write a sentence about Rita's spending habits.

_____

_____

3. List three reasons why Rita is having problems managing her money.

_____

_____

_____

4. List the changes that Rita should make in her spending habits.

_____

_____

_____

5. Rita has take-home pay of $484.00 every two weeks. She has no cash on hand. Help her prepare her budget for two weeks. Decide how much she will spend on her needs and wants. Use the budget record form below. Remember that her total expenses cannot be more than her total income.

Budget Record Form

Cash on Hand:

Estimated Income (Salary/Wages):

TOTAL ESTIMATED CASH:

Estimated Expenses:

TOTAL ESTIMATED EXPENSES $

Total Estimated Cash $

Total Estimated Expenses —

CASH ON HAND
(end of Budget Period)

Case 5

Help Jill Ly prepare a budget plan for the pay period of April 4 to April 17. Jill will have the following income. Write these figures on the budget record form on page 42.

Cash on Hand—$20.00   Salary—$154.78

Jill also expects to have the following expenses. Write them on the budget record form.

Room and Board—$50.00   Savings—$20.00

Clothes—$30.00   Entertainment—$25.00

Grooming Needs—$10.00   Bus Fare—$20.00

Miscellaneous Items—$15.00

A Help Jill prepare her budget plan. Complete the form on page 42. Remember that her budget is for two weeks. The total of her estimated expenses must be less than her estimated income.

B Write the answers to the following questions about Jill's budget.

1. How much is Jill's estimated income? _____

2. How much are Jill's estimated expenses? _____

3. How much money does Jill expect to have at the end of the budget period?

_____

4. What is Jill's take-home pay? _____

Jill Would Like to Buy New CDs for Her CD Player

Budget Record Form

_____

_____

_____

Cash on Hand:

Estimated Income (Salary/Wages):

TOTAL ESTIMATED CASH:

Estimated Expenses:

TOTAL ESTIMATED EXPENSES $

Total Estimated Cash $ _____

Total Estimated Expenses — _____

CASH ON HAND
(end of Budget Period)

Case 6

Help Mike McBride prepare his budget plan for the pay period of October 13 to October 27. Mike will have the following income. Write these figures on the budget record form on page 44.

Cash on Hand—$21.78   Salary—$336.48

Mike also expects the following expenses. Write them on the budget record form.

Rent—$70.00   Motorcycle Payment—$154.46

Savings—$20.00   Lunches—$20.00

Entertainment—$35.00   Motorcycle Expenses—$40.00

Miscellaneous Items—$10.00   Personal Needs—$5.00

A Help Mike prepare his budget plan for a two-week period. Complete the form on page 44. Remember that his total expenses must not be more than his total estimated income.

B Write the answers to the following questions about Mike's budget.

1. How much is Mike's estimated income? _____

2. How much are Mike's estimated expenses? _____

3. How much money does Mike expect to have at the end of the budget period?

_____

4. What is Mike's take-home pay? _____

How Much Does Mike Spend on His Motorcycle?

Budget Record Form

_____

_____

_____

Cash on Hand:

Estimated Income (Salary/Wages):

TOTAL ESTIMATED CASH:

Estimated Expenses:

TOTAL ESTIMATED EXPENSES $

Total Estimated Cash $ _____

Total Estimated Expenses —   _____

CASH ON HAND
(end of Budget Period)

Review Unit 3

Help Robert and Juanita Valez prepare their budget plan for the pay period of May 1 to May 15. Mr. and Mrs. Valez will have the following income. Write these figures on the budget record form on page 46.

Robert Valez's salary—$642.25   Juanita Valez's salary—$448.26

Cash on Hand—$25.00

Robert and Juanita Valez also expect to have the following expenses. Write them on the budget record form.

Mortgage Payment—$375.00   Savings—$20.00

Furniture Payment—$142.00   Utility Bills—$100.00

Credit Card Payment—$175.00   Groceries—$150.00

Children's Allowance—$40.00   Grooming Needs—$15.00

Entertainment—$40.00   Miscellaneous Items—$30.00

A Help Robert and Juanita Valez prepare their budget plan for a two-week period. Complete the form on page 46.

B Write the answers to the following questions about Robert and Juanita Valez's budget.

1. How much is Robert and Juanita Valez's estimated income? _____

2. How much are Robert and Juanita Valez's estimated expenses? _____

3. How much money do Robert and Juanita Valez expect to have at the end of the budget period? _____

4. What is the total take-home pay for the Valez family? _____

**The Budget Includes
a Furniture Payment**

Budget Record Form

_____

_____

_____

Cash on Hand:

Estimated Income (Salary/Wages):

TOTAL ESTIMATED CASH:

Estimated Expenses:

TOTAL ESTIMATED EXPENSES | $

Total Estimated Cash $ _____

Total Estimated Expenses — _____

CASH ON HAND
(end of Budget Period)

Fixed and Variable Expenses

All expenses are not the same. In this unit, you are going to learn about several different types. The following terms are important in helping you learn about expenses.

Terms to Know	
Estimate	to guess how much an item will cost
Fixed expenses	items for a specific amount of money that must be paid on a given date
Variable expenses	items that do not occur regularly in a budget. The amount of money spent for these items often varies.
Percentage	the number or amount stated as percent, or as part of one hundred

Study the examples of fixed and variable expenses in the chart below.

Fixed Expenses

1. Rent or mortgage payment
2. Utilities: electricity, water, gas, or oil
3. Insurance payments: car, life, or hospitalization
4. Credit card payments
5. Working expenses: transportation, car repairs, bus fare
6. Installment payments: furniture or car

Variable Expenses

1. Food
2. Medical expenses not covered by hospitalization
3. Household repairs: appliances or plumbing
4. Clothing
5. Transportation: gasoline, car repairs, bus fare
6. Recreation: vacations, hobbies
7. Entertainment: movies, sports
8. Miscellaneous items: magazines or newspapers, postage, gifts

Both fixed and variable expenses affect a person's budget. A person must have money to pay for fixed expenses during a budget period. These expenses are needs that a person must have to live. What would happen to a person if he or she did not pay fixed expenses each month? Someone could lose his or her house if the mortgage was not paid. Insurance coverage would be dropped if a person did not pay the payments when they were due. Fixed expenses must be paid on time.

Variable expenses

Variable expenses are different from fixed expenses. First of all, the amount of a variable expense may change during each budget period. Most of our wants fall into the variable expense category. Such expenses can be reduced or postponed. Someone can spend less money for clothes. A vacation can be postponed to a later date. One can do without a new television or get a brand that is cheaper. Someone can buy a new television set this year and a stereo next year. A person does have to eat, but he or she can decide what food items to purchase. One can save money by buying chicken instead of steak. It is important to make decisions about variable expenses so that there will be enough money to pay for one's needs or fixed expenses.

Periodic fixed and variable expenses

Some fixed and variable expenses occur at different times. They can cost much money. Many people also set aside small amounts of money during each budget period to pay for large bills that they know they will have to pay by a certain time. People can also plan ahead for gifts, vacations, and other items. Let us see how Joey Mandez saves money for certain fixed expenses.

Joey's estimated fixed and variable expenses

Joey has many variable expenses. He does not always spend money for them during each pay period. He saves some money each pay period to pay for these items. He gets paid twice a month.

1. Joey deposits $20 each pay period into his savings account for his vacation. He will have $480 to spend on his vacation next summer.

2. Joey estimates that he spends about $240 for gifts each year. If he saves $9.50 each pay period, he will have $228 for gifts.

3. Joey estimates that he spends $500 for clothes each year. If he saves $20 each pay period, he will have about this amount of money for clothes.

4. Joey's employer pays for his health insurance. This insurance does not pay for all his medical, dental, and medicine expenses. He estimates that he pays about $300 for these expenses each year. If he saves $24 one pay period out of each month, he will have enough money for medical expenses.

Dividing Net Income

How much money should people set aside from their net income to pay for their fixed and variable expenses? The following chart shows the average percentage of net earnings that should be set aside.

A Pie Graph Can Show How Income Is Divided

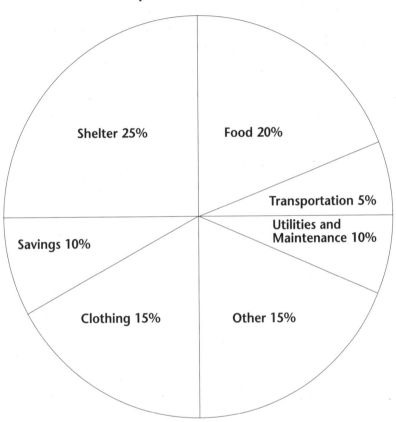

Shelter 25%

Food 20%

Transportation 5%

Utilities and Maintenance 10%

Savings 10%

Clothing 15%

Other 15%

This type of chart is often called a circle graph or a pie chart. It shows parts of a whole. In this case, the chart shows how income is divided up into different areas or expenses. What do the percentages on this chart mean? *Percent* means per hundred, or a hundredth part. The symbol % is used to show percent. For each $1.00 of net earnings (or take-home pay), the following amounts should be spent in each area.

Dividing Net Income

Shelter	$.25
Food	.20
Transportation	.05
Clothing	.15
Savings	.10
Utilities	.10
Other	.15

You have just seen how one can pay for expenses by dividing up net income. Percents can also be used to figure out budget expenses. Look at Denise Gordon's budget. She is a student and works part time as a salesperson at Tracey's Department Store. Denise's monthly income is $768. She has already decided on the percentages for each expense in her monthly budget. She is ready for the next step.

 Read the list of expense items from Denise's budget below. Study the example. Then help her figure out the dollar amount for each of her expenses.

Example: 17% for room and board

17% = .17

```
   $768
x   .17
   5376
   768
$130.56 for room and board
```

Denise's income is $768. Of that total, she will need to spend 17%, or $130.56, on room and board.

12% savings	14% clothing	5% medical	8% lunches	9% entertainment
1. $ _____	2. $ _____	3. $ _____	4. $ _____	5. $ _____
10% transportation	4% computer class	3% gift fund	11% insurance	7% miscellaneous
6. $ _____	7. $ _____	8. $ _____	9. $ _____	10. $ _____

Alberto Ruez is also working on his budget. He works as a driver for the Apex Parcel Service. His monthly net income is $1,584. He is preparing a monthly budget.

■ Read the list of expense items from Alberto's budget. Help him figure out how much of his income he will need for each expense item. Study the first example. Then figure out the dollar amount for each of Alberto's expenses.

Example: 22% for rent
             22% = .22

             $1,584
             x .22
             3168
             3168
             $348.48 for rent

             Alberto's income is $1,584. Of that total, he will need to spend 22%, or $348.48 on rent.

20% food	6% medical	7% lunches	16% car expenses
1. $ _____	2. $ _____	3. $ _____	4. $ _____

10% utilities	10% insurance	9% miscellaneous
5. $ _____	6. $ _____	7. $ _____

The following graph shows how the Alwine family spends its monthly income of $2,256. Notice the different percentages that are spent in each area.

This Graph Shows the Alwine Family Budget

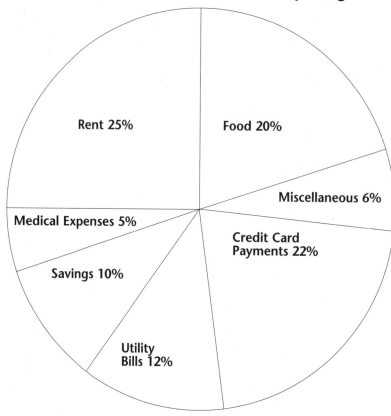

Rent 25%   Food 20%

Miscellaneous 6%

Medical Expenses 5%

Credit Card
Payments 22%

Savings 10%

Utility
Bills 12%

Study the above graph. Use the graph to figure out how much money the Alwine family spends for each of the following expenses. Look at the example. Then figure out the dollar amounts that are spent for each expense.

Example: How much money is spent for rent? 25% = .25
        $2,256
        x   .25
        11280
        4512
        $564.00

1. How much money is spent for food? _____

2. How much money is spent for medical expenses? _____

3. How much money is spent for utility bills? _____

4. How much money is deposited into savings? _____

5. How much money is spent for credit card payments? _____

6. How much money is spent for miscellaneous? _____

Comparing Income and Expenses

Look at the following case history. Reuben and Ana Pabon's monthly net income is $1,048.00. They have used the same percentages as those given on the chart on page 49. Notice how the Pabons budget their income.

Shelter	$1,048 x 25% (.25) = $262.00
Food	$1,048 x 20% (.20) = $209.60
Transportation	$1,048 x 05% (.05) = $52.40
Clothing	$1,048 x 15% (.15) = $157.20
Savings	$1,048 x 10% (.10) = $104.80
Utilities	$1,048 x 10% (.10) = $104.80
Miscellaneous	$1,048 x 15% (.15) = $157.20
Total expenses	$1,048.00

Inflation and net family income

Inflation is making it difficult for the Pabons to spend their income as suggested on the chart. For example, 25% for shelter allows them $262.00, yet their actual rent has risen to $300.00. Also, 20% for food allows them $209.60, but they are actually spending $250 for food. How do they make ends meet? They can do without many variable expense items. They could choose not to take a vacation. They could spend less money for recreation. Savings in these areas will give them more money to spend on essentials such as food and rent.

The Pabons find it difficult to live on one paycheck. Ana decides to take a part-time job as a bank teller. Her added income can help pay for important fixed and variable expenses. The Pabons, like many other families, have become a two-paycheck family. The additional income will give them more money to spend on their wants as well as their needs.

Can Reuben and Ana Pabon Afford a Car?

UNIT 4

The following people are planning their fixed and variable expenses for their budgets. Such expenses can be figured for a period of one year.

Example: Harry is saving $8.00 each week for medical expenses. There are 52 weeks in one year.

$8.00 x 52 = $416.00

If he saves $8.00 every week, Harry can save $416.00 in one year for his medical expenses.

◼ Figure out how much money each person will have in one year.

1. Janet is saving $10.00 each week for gifts. How much can she save in a year?

   _____

2. Raoul is saving $25.00 each week for a car. How much will he save in one year?

   _____

3. Linda is saving $17.00 every two weeks for clothes. How much will she save in one year?

   _____

4. Jim deposits $9.50 each week into his savings account. How much will be in his savings account at the end of one year? _____

5. Dorene is saving $15.00 every two weeks for her vacation. How much will she save for her vacation in one year? _____

Review Unit 4

The following people are planning their fixed and variable expenses for their budgets. They would like to estimate how much they can save in one year.

■ Figure out how much money each person will save in one year.

1. Carmen is saving $9.00 each week for car insurance. How much can she save for her insurance in one year? _____

2. Jean is saving $13.00 every two weeks for holiday gifts. How much money can she save for gifts in one year? _____

3. Bill is saving $75.00 each month for a down payment on a car. How much money will he have for a down payment in one year? _____

4. Toni is saving $16.00 every two weeks for clothes. How much money will she save for clothes in one year? _____

5. John is saving $8.50 each week for a camera. How much money can he save for a camera in one year? _____

6. Barbara is saving $17.00 each week for her vacation. How much can she save for her vacation in one year? _____

7. Elizabeth's monthly income is $2,455.00. She spends 22% of her income on rent. What is her monthly rent payment? _____

8. Blake spends 6% of his monthly income on train fare, and he spends 4% of his income on car maintenance. His weekly take-home pay is $490.00. How much does Blake spend on transportation each month? _____

9. Tawana has two part-time jobs. One job pays $795.00 per month, and the other job pays $1,015.00 per month. Each month, Tawana spends 5% of her income on pet care products and grooming for her two cocker spaniels. How much does she spend on pet care each month? _____

10. Chris has monthly take-home pay of $1,880.00. Each month he spends a certain percentage of his income on the items listed below. How much does he spend each month on these items?

25% rent	7% savings	20% food	14% car payment
_____	_____	_____	_____

Test Units 3–4

A John Williams needs to plan his budget for the pay period May 14 to May 28. His income is as follows:

Cash on hand—$13.64   Salary—$315.63

1. Make a budget record form like the one on page 46. Record John's expenses on it. His expenses are as follows:

    Savings $20.00   Grooming $14.00

    Rent $103.00   New Clothing $43.00

    Bus Fare $9.00   Credit Card Payments $65.00

    Entertainment $17.00   Miscellaneous $4.00

    Medical Expenses $18.00   Utility Bills $28.00

2. How much is John's estimated income? _____

3. How much are John's estimated expenses? _____

4. How much cash on hand does John expect to have at the end of the budget period?

    _____

B Lucille Thompson is a construction worker. Her monthly income is $1,775.00. The following shows the percentage of her income that is spent in each category.

    Savings 8%   Transportation 18%

    Clothing 10%   Vacation 12%

    Medical 9%   Credit Cards 14%

    Lunches 5%   Insurance 16%

    Entertainment 5%   Miscellaneous 3%

What is the specific amount of her monthly income that she will need to spend in each category?

5. Savings _____   10. Transportation _____

6. Clothing _____   11. Vacation _____

7. Medical _____   12. Credit Cards _____

8. Lunches _____   13. Insurance _____

9. Entertainment _____ 14. Miscellaneous _____

Examining a Budget Plan

Read the terms listed below. Understanding these terms will help you work with budget record and cash record forms.

Terms to Know	
Budget	a plan for how a person will spend her or his money during the budget period
Cash record	a form that shows daily how money was spent during the budget period
Cash on hand	the amount of money a person has at the beginning and end of a budget period. This money can be added to the estimated income to be used during the next budget period.
Balance column	a column on the cash record form that shows the cash on hand at the end of the budget period
Income column	a column on the cash record form that shows the amount of money received during the budget period

Joey Mandez's budget record form

In Unit 2 you studied Joey Mandez's budget record forms. Copies of these forms can be found on page 58. Joey found that he could not live within his first budget. His estimated expenses were more than his estimated income.

Joey had to revise his budget. First, he examined his spending habits. He used decision-making skills to change his list of wants and needs. He learned that his estimated expenses could not be more than his estimated income. Look at Joey's second budget plan. His estimated expenses are now equal to his estimated income.

Joey's budget is only a start for using good money management skills. He must make sure that his budget plan works. He must live within his budget.

Budget Record Form

Joey Mandez
For Pay Period March 16 to March 31, 1998

Cash on Hand:	-45 37
Estimated Income (Salary/Wages):	285 87
TOTAL ESTIMATED CASH:	240 50

Estimated Expenses:

Room and Board	50 00
Lunches	30 00
Bus Fare	25 00
Savings	30 00
Vacation Fund	20 00
Medical Expenses	15 00
Entertainment	20 00
Stereo Fund	5 00
Grooming Needs	20 00
Clothing Fund	20 00
Miscellaneous Expenses	5 50
TOTAL ESTIMATED EXPENSES	$ 240 50

Total Estimated Cash	$ 240 50
Total Estimated Expenses	— 240 50
CASH ON HAND (end of Budget Period)	0 00

Budget Record Form

Joey Mandez
For Pay Period March 1 to March 15, 1998

Cash on Hand:	8 76
Estimated Income (Salary/Wages):	285 87
TOTAL ESTIMATED CASH:	294 63

Estimated Expenses:

New Clothes	50 00
Entertainment	30 00
Vacation Fund	30 00
Lunches	50 00
Gifts	20 00
Bus Fare	20 00
Room & Board	50 00
Payment for Dental Exam	70 00
Miscellaneous Expenses	20 00
TOTAL ESTIMATED EXPENSES	$ 340 00

Total Estimated Cash	$ 294 63
Total Estimated Expenses	— 340 00
CASH ON HAND (end of Budget Period)	— 45 37

Cash Record Information

A cash record helps a person follow a budget plan. It also shows how a person spends money during the budget period. Remember that Joey Mandez's first budget did not balance. He overspent by $45.37. His second budget started with a minus cash on hand of $45.37. He needed to make up the money that he had overspent on his first budget. His second budget is included on the cash record shown on page 60. Joey has learned how to balance his budget. Keeping a cash record showed him how his money was being spent.

Cash Record Information

1. The name of the person is given on line 1.

2. The date of the budget period is written on line 2.

3. The date column is shown on line 3, column A. This column shows when money is received and when money is spent.

4. The explanation column is on line 3, column B. This column shows the source of any income. It also describes the items on which money was spent.

5. The cash/income column is on line 3, column C. This column shows the amount of any cash on hand at the beginning of the budget period. It also shows any income received during the budget period.

6. The expense column is given on line 3, column D. This column shows the amount of any money spent during the budget period.

7. The balance column is on line 3, column E. This column shows the new balance after any money is received or spent. The last figure tells you how much you can still spend in the budget period and yet stay within your budget.

Cash on hand

The balance column in the cash record shows important information. It shows how much cash on hand a person has at any time during the budget period. The amount of money in this balance column becomes larger when income is received. The amount of money in this balance column becomes smaller when money is spent. Looking at the last figure in the balance column tells you if you are staying within your budget. In his cash record, Joey kept to his budget exactly. He knew when he had spent all the money that his budget allowed him to spend. The use of a cash record helped Joey not overspend in this budget period.

CASH RECORD

		A	B	C		D		E	
1		*Joey Mandez*							
2		*March 16 to March 31, 1998*							
3		**Date**		**Explanation**	**Cash/Income**		**Expense**		**Balance**	
4		*Mar*	*16*	*Cash on Hand*	*− 45*	*37*			*− 45*	*37*
5			*16*	*Salary*	*285*	*87*			*240*	*50*
6			*17*	*Room and Board*			*50*	*00*	*190*	*50*
7			*17*	*Lunches*			*15*	*00*	*175*	*50*
8			*17*	*Bus Fare*			*12*	*50*	*163*	*00*
9			*17*	*Savings*			*30*	*00*	*133*	*00*
10			*17*	*Vacation Fund*			*20*	*00*	*113*	*00*
11			*19*	*Dentist*			*10*	*00*	*103*	*00*
12			*20*	*Movie*			*3*	*50*	*99*	*50*
13			*20*	*Toiletries*			*11*	*24*	*88*	*26*
14			*21*	*Concert*			*10*	*25*	*78*	*01*
15			*23*	*Lunches*			*15*	*00*	*63*	*01*
16			*24*	*Stereo Fund*			*5*	*00*	*58*	*01*
17			*24*	*Dinner*			*6*	*25*	*51*	*76*
18			*25*	*Medicine*			*5*	*00*	*46*	*76*
19			*25*	*Bus Fare*			*12*	*50*	*34*	*26*
20			*25*	*Clothing Fund*			*20*	*00*	*14*	*26*
21			*27*	*Haircut*			*8*	*76*	*5*	*50*
22			*29*	*Miscellaneous*			*5*	*50*	*0*	*00*
23										
24										
25										

Money Management

Joey Mandez is now an experienced money manager. He can live within his budget each pay period. His expenses are not more than his income. He tries to have some money, or cash on hand, left over for the next budget period. He keeps a cash record to show how his money was spent.

You are going to look at several of Joey's budget record and cash record forms. You will notice that the ending balances may differ. That difference occurs because a budget record form shows the *estimated* amounts of money in round numbers, and a cash record shows the *itemized* amounts of money in the actual dollars and cents spent.

Study Joey's cash record shown on page 62. Joey's second May cash record begins with a cash on hand of $18.76. The amounts of some items (salary, for example) are the same as they were in his second March cash record. He also spent the same amount for room and board: $50.00. Other items were different; for example, grooming needs and medicine. Can you see other items on which Joey spent different amounts during the periods of these two cash records?

Take a closer look at the form on page 62 to see how Joey used the different parts of this cash record. This cash record is for the budget period of May 17 to May 31.

People Can Become Experienced Money Managers

CASH RECORD

1			*Joey Mandez*							
2			*May 17 to May 31, 1998*							

	A		B	C		D		E	
3	Date		Explanation	Cash/Income		Expense		Balance	
4	May	17	Cash on Hand	18	76			18	76
5		17	Salary	285	87			304	63
6		17	Room and Board			50	00	254	63
7		17	Savings			30	00	224	63
8		17	Vacation Fund			20	00	204	63
9		18	Lunches			20	00	184	63
10		18	Bus Fare			20	00	164	63
11		18	Gift Fund			9	50	155	13
12		18	Stereo Fund			2	00	153	13
13		19	Medical Fund			15	00	138	13
14		20	Shaving Supplies			9	62	128	51
15		20	Clothing Fund			20	00	108	51
16		22	Dental Supplies			6	56	101	95
17		24	Miscellaneous Items			5	00	96	95
18		25	Grooming Needs			11	53	85	42
19		25	Dinner and Movie			10	90	74	52
20		25	Lunches			20	00	54	52
21		25	Bus Fare			20	00	34	52
22		28	Miscellaneous Items			15	00	19	52
23		29	Bowling and Snack			7	42	12	10
24			Totals	304	63	292	53	12	10
25									

Completing a Cash Record

Several steps are involved in recording information on the cash record. Look at how Joey Mandez entered his actual income and expenses on this form.

1. Look at the figure for cash on hand at the beginning of the budget period. This information was recorded on line 4 in columns C and E.

	A			B	C		D		E	
3	Date			Explanation	Cash/Income		Expense		Balance	
4	May	17		Cash on Hand	18	76			18	76

2. The income, or money received, was recorded on line 5 in column C. The income on line 5 in column C was added to the balance on line 4 in column E.

$ 18.76 Cash on hand
+285.87 Salary
$304.63 New balance

$304.63 was the new balance from which expenses will be deducted.

	A			B	C		D		E	
3	Date			Explanation	Cash/Income		Expense		Balance	
4	May	17		Cash on Hand	18	76			18	76
5		17		Salary	285	87			304	63

3. Expenses during the budget period were recorded on lines 6 through 23. Each expense listed in column D was subtracted from the balance on the line above it to get the current balance.

$304.63 Balance after income was added
– 50.00 First expense recorded on line 6
$254.63 Current balance after first expense was subtracted

	A			B	C		D		E	
3	Date			Explanation	Cash/Income		Expense		Balance	
4	May	17		Cash on Hand	18	76			18	76
5		16		Salary	285	87			304	63
6		17		Room and Board			50	00	254	63

Information must be entered correctly in a cash record. Look at how Joey recorded some of the information in his cash record. (Lines 4, 5, and 6 were discussed on page 63.)

■ Write Joey's expenses on his cash record form. Use lines 7 through 13. Remember to record each item on the correct line and column. Find the current balance after each expense.

Line 7 On May 17, Joey deposited $30.00 into his savings account. Record this information on line 7 under expenses. Subtract this amount to find the new balance.

Line 8 On May 17, Joey deposited $20.00 into his vacation fund. Record this information on line 8. Find the next balance.

Line 9 On May 18, Joey set aside $20.00 for lunches. Record this information on line 9. Find the next balance.

Line 10 On May 18, Joey set aside $20.00 for bus fare. Record this information on line 10. Find the next balance.

Line 11 On May 18, Joey set aside $9.50 for his gift fund. Record this amount on line 11. Find the next balance.

Line 12 On May 18, Joey set aside $2.00 for his stereo fund. Record this amount on line 12. Find the next balance.

Line 13 On May 19, Joey set aside $15.00 for his medical fund. Record this amount on line 13. Find the final balance.

	A	B	C		D		E	
3	Date	Explanation	Cash/Income		Expense		Balance	
4	May 17	Cash on Hand	18	76			18	76
5	17	Salary	285	87			304	63
6	17	Room and Board			50	00	254	63
7								
8								
9								
10								
11								
12								
13								

Closing a Cash Record

People use cash record forms to follow their budget plan. They must make sure that all the information is correct in the income, expense, and balance columns. They list all the expenses for the budget period. Then they must close the cash record. Here are the steps that Joey followed to prove the accuracy of his cash record.

1. He drew a line with a red pencil underneath the line for the last entry of the budget period. The date of this last entry was May 29. Notice the double line under line 23 in the example below.

22							
23	29	Bowling and Snack				7 42	12 10
24							

2. He added the numbers in the cash/income column and in the expense column. He wrote the totals in small penciled figures underneath the line that he drew under line 23. Look at the example below.

23	29	Bowling and Snack				7 42	12 10
24				304 63	292 53		12 10
25							

3. On a separate sheet of paper, he listed the temporary totals of the cash record.

$ 18.76	Cash on hand on May 17, the first day of his budget period
+285.87	Salary
$304.63	Total cash/income
− 292.53	Expenses
$12.10	Final balance as of May 29

Notice that May 31 is the last day of the budget period, but the cash record was closed on May 29. Joey did not have any new expenses after that date.

4. Next, Joey proved that he subtracted each expense from every balance correctly. When he subtracted his total expenses of $292.53 from his total cash/income of $304.63, he had a balance of $12.10. Look at line 23. The last figure in the balance column for May 29 is also $12.10. If these two figures did not match, then Joey would have to find the mistake in his calculations and correct it. All of Joey's math must be correct before he can close his cash record.

5. Joey closed his cash record since he proved that the totals in his cash record were correct. Then Joey wrote the following information on line 24.

   a. He wrote the word *Totals* in the explanation column.

   b. He wrote the pencil totals in ink on line 24.

   c. He wrote the final balance figure, $12.10, in ink.

All of these steps are shown in the example below. Look at it carefully.

23	29	Bowling and Snack				7	42	12	10
24		Totals	304 63 / 304 63		292 53 / 292 53		12 10 / 12 10

6. Finally, Joey drew a line with a red pencil underneath the date, cash/income, and balance columns to show that his cash record for this budget period had been closed. Notice the double-ruled line under line 24. Joey's new cash on hand balance is now $12.10. This figure is the amount of money that he has to start his new budget plan.

Using a cash record

Help Joey Mandez complete his cash record for the budget period of June 1 to June 15. Look at the cash record form on page 68. Figure out the balance for each item. Close the cash record at the end of the budget period. Follow steps 1 through 6 as given above.

Using a Cash Record: June 1–15

Joey must prove the accuracy of his cash record at the end of the budget period. Help him close his cash record for June 1 to June 15. Remember the steps for closing a cash record. Complete the form on page 68.

1. Complete the figures in the balance column. Draw a red line under the last entry.

2. Add the figures in the cash/income column and the expense column. Write these totals in pencil. Also write, in pencil, the last figure in the balance column.

3. Prove the accuracy of Joey's temporary totals.

    a. What is the cash on hand on June 1? Look at line 4 of the cash record.

    _____

    b. What is Joey's income? _____

    c. What is his total cash/income? _____

    d. What are his total expenses? _____

    e. What is his final balance on June 15? _____

4. Does the final balance agree with the balance for the temporary totals in the cash record? If they do not agree, you must look for an error and correct it.

5. Write the word *totals* in the explanation column. Write your penciled totals in ink. Write the final balance figure in ink.

6. Close the cash record for the budget period. Draw a double-ruled line underneath the totals on line 22.

You have now closed Joey's cash record for June 1–15.

Calculators Can Help You Close a Cash Record

CASH RECORD

Joey Mandez
June 1 to June 15, 1998

		B	C Cash/Income		D Expense		E Balance	
A Date		**Explanation**						
June	1	Cash on Hand	12	10			12	10
	1	Salary	295	57			307	67
	1	Savings			25	00	282	67
	1	Vacation Fund			20	00	262	67
	3	Room and Board			50	00		
	3	Movie			4	00		
	4	Lunches			20	00		
	4	Bus Fare			20	00		
	5	Eye Exam			35	00		
	6	Gift Book			8	50		
	6	Grooming Needs			11	46		
	6	Dinner			12	50		
	7	Contribution			10	50		
	8	Movie			4	00		
	9	Shoes			29	88		
	11	Lunches			20	00		
	11	Bus Fare			20	00		
	15	Miscellaneous			3	52		
		Totals						

Using a Cash Record: June 16–30

Help Joey Mandez complete his next cash record. Look at the cash record form on page 70. Study the portion of the form that has already been completed. Follow the steps that you have learned for using a cash record. Close the cash record at the end of the budget period.

1. Complete the figures in the balance column. Draw a red line under the last entry.

2. Add the figures in the cash/income column and the expense column. Write these totals in pencil. Also write, in pencil, the last figure in the balance column.

3. Prove the accuracy of Joey's temporary totals.

   a. What is the cash on hand on June 16? Look at line 4 of the cash record.

   b. What is Joey's income? _____

   c. What is his total cash/income? _____

   d. What are his total expenses? _____

   e. What is his final balance on June 30? _____

4. Does the final balance agree with the balance for the temporary totals in the cash record? If they do not agree, you must look for an error and correct it.

5. Is the word *totals* written in the explanation column? Write your penciled totals in ink. Write the final balance figure in ink.

6. Close the cash record for the budget period. Draw a double-ruled line underneath the totals on line 23.

Check to see that you have completed all of the steps correctly. You have now closed Joey's cash record for June 16–30.

CASH RECORD

Joey Mandez

June 16 to June 30, 1998

	A		B	C		D		E	
	Date		Explanation	Cash/Income		Expense		Balance	
4	June	16	Cash on Hand	13	31			13	31
5		16	Salary	295	57			308	88
6		16	Savings			25	00	283	88
7		16	Vacation Fund			20	00	263	88
8		17	Room and Board			50	00		
9		18	Lunches			20	00		
10		18	Bus Fare			20	00		
11		19	Dinner			11	50		
12		20	Movie			6	50		
13		20	Clothing Fund			25	00		
14		21	Medicine			12	00		
15		22	Jacket			30	00		
16		22	Gift			5	25		
17		24	Books			8	00		
18		25	Stereo Fund			2	00		
19		26	Lunches			20	00		
20		26	Bus Fare			20	00		
21		30	Miscellaneous			4	76		
22		30	Dinner			10	50		
23			Totals						
24									
25									

The Cash Record: Terms to Know

A Read the following list carefully. Choose the correct term for each sentence. Write your answers on the lines.

- expense column
- cash record
- cash/income column
- balance column
- cash on hand
- budget
- explanation column

1. A _____ is a plan for how a person will spend future income.

2. _____ is the amount of money that a person has left at the end of the budget period. This money can be added to the income for the next period.

3. The _____ is a form that shows how money was spent during the budget period.

4. The _____ shows the amount of money that was received during the budget period.

5. The _____ describes how money was received or spent in the cash record.

6. The _____ shows the amount of money spent during the budget period.

7. The _____ shows cash on hand after money is received or spent.

B Match the definitions in Column 2 with the terms in Column 1.

Column 1

_____ 8. Cash on hand

_____ 9. Cash/income column

_____ 10. Balance column

_____ 11. Budget

_____ 12. Expense column

_____ 13. Cash record

_____ 14. Explanation column

Column 2

a. Shows how much money was spent during the budget period

b. The amount of cash a person has at the beginning and end of the budget period

c. Shows the amount of money on hand and received during the budget period

d. A form that shows how much money was spent during the budget period

e. Shows cash on hand after money is received or spent

f. Describes how money was received or spent on the cash recorded

g. A plan for spending future income

C Define the following terms. Use complete sentences.

15. Budget _____

_____

16. Cash record _____

_____

17. Explanation column _____

_____

18. Income column _____

_____

19. Expense column _____

_____

20. Balance column _____

_____

21. Cash on hand _____

_____

Budgets Can Help You Save Money

Review Unit 5

A Read the following list of terms. Choose the term that will complete each sentence. Write your answers on the lines.

• needs	• balance	• decision making	• cash on hand
• budget	• salary	• temporary totals	• fixed expenses
• income	• values	• variable expenses	• cash record
• inflation	• wants	• manage	• expenses

1. A _____ is the money that a person earns by working.

2. _____ is the amount of money that a person has at the beginning and end of a budget period.

3. _____ means that it takes more money to buy an item than it did previously.

4. _____ are items or services that must be paid for.

5. _____ are things that people like but that they can live without.

6. A _____ is a plan of how a person will spend his or her income.

7. _____ are the way that people feel about important matters.

8. _____ are specific amounts of money that must be paid on a certain date.

9. _____ are things that a person must have in order to live.

10. A _____ shows how a person spends his or her money during a budget period.

11. _____ do not occur regularly in a budget.

12. _____ occurs when a person considers all possible choices when solving a problem.

13. _____ are figures written in pencil on a cash record.

14. Another name for salary is _____ .

15. To _____ money, a person must live within a budget each pay period.

16. The _____ is the amount of money left after each expense has been subtracted.

B Match the definition in Column 2 with the correct term in Column 1.

Column 1	Column 2

_____ 17. Inflation

_____ 18. Cash record

_____ 19. Needs

_____ 20. Budget

_____ 21. Values

_____ 22. Expenses

_____ 23. Decision making

_____ 24. Salary

_____ 25. Wants

_____ 26. Balance

_____ 27. Fixed expenses

_____ 28. Variable expenses

a. Items that people need for everyday living

b. Thinking of all the choices when solving a problem

c. More money is now needed to buy an item that once cost less money

d. Items that people like but can live without

e. Money earned by a person

f. A plan of how a person expects to spend estimated income

g. The amount of money that a person has left after spending money

h. The way people feel about important things

i. Items that a person spends money for during a budget period

j. An itemized record that shows how money is spent during a budget period

k. Budget items that are not paid regularly

l. Budget items that must be paid regularly

C Look at the list of scrambled words. Study the example. Then write the correct spelling of each word.

Example: ATSWN _____wants_____

29. CNIMOE _____

30. DRCERO _____

31. GETDUB _____

32. SENEEPXS _____

33. IOTLAFINN _____

34. BECNALA _____

35. EDATIMETS _____

36. METYRAROP _____

37. YNEOM _____

38. AVSEUL _____

D The following words are hidden in the puzzle below. They are placed horizontally, vertically, and diagonally. Some words are spelled backwards. Circle each word that you find. Put a check mark after each word in the list after you have circled the word.

- budget
- expenses
- plan
- needs
- earnings
- cash
- temporary

- totals
- balance
- estimated
- record
- period
- salary
- income

R	E	C	O	R	D	H	S	A	C
T	E	M	P	O	R	A	R	Y	E
E	A	B	N	E	E	D	S	P	S
X	R	E	I	N	C	O	M	E	T
P	N	C	P	T	U	V	S	R	I
E	I	N	X	L	D	U	L	I	M
N	N	A	Y	M	A	Y	A	O	A
S	G	L	Z	P	D	N	T	D	T
E	S	A	L	A	R	Y	O	C	E
S	B	B	U	D	G	E	T	E	D

E Write the answers to the following questions. Use complete sentences.

39. What is inflation? _____

_____

40. Give an example of inflation. _____

_____

41. List two ways in which a person can deal with inflation. _____

_____

42. What is a budget? _____

_____

43. What is a cash record? _____

_____

44. What are needs? _____

_____

45. What are wants? _____

_____

46. Which are more important, needs or wants? Explain your answer. _____

_____

47. Why is it important to set up goals for budget planning? _____

_____

48. What are values? _____

_____

49. How do values influence the way in which a person spends money? _____

_____

50. Why is it important to use decision-making skills in planning a budget? _____

_____

51. What must a person do to make sure that her or his budget will balance? _____

_____

52. List two things that a person can do if the budget does not balance. _____

_____

53. What information does the balance column have at any given time? _____

_____

Victor Won's Budget

Lesson 1

UNIT 6

Help Victor Won prepare his budget plan for the pay period of October 15 to October 31. Victor will have the following income.

Cash on hand—$20.75   Salary—$615.52

Victor expects to have the following expenses.

Rent $295.00   Insurance $50.00

Car Expenses $40.00   Food $150.00

Vacation Fund $20.00   Medical Expenses $10.00

Utility Bills $40.00   Miscellaneous Expenses $20.00

 A Help Victor prepare his budget plan for the two-week pay period. Use the form on page 78. Allow enough money to pay for all of his needs and at least some of his wants. Remember that his expenses must not be more than his total income.

B Write the answers to the following questions about Victor's budget plan.

1. What is Victor's estimated income? _____

2. How much cash on hand does Victor have at the beginning of the budget period? _____

3. What is Victor's total estimated cash at the beginning of the budget period? _____

4. How much does Victor pay for rent, utility bills, and food?

   _____

5. What are Victor's estimated expenses? _____

6. How much cash on hand does Victor expect to have at the end of his budget period? _____

UNIT 6 *BUDGETS AND CASH RECORDS* **77**

Budget Record Form

_____

_____

_____

Cash on Hand:

Estimated Income (Salary/Wages):

TOTAL ESTIMATED CASH:

Estimated Expenses:

TOTAL ESTIMATED EXPENSES $

Total Estimated Cash $ _____

Total Estimated Expenses — _____

CASH ON HAND
(end of Budget Period)

Victor's Cash Record

Victor Won is also keeping a cash record for his budget period. Help Victor record the following items in his cash record.

 Read the information below. Record each item on the correct line and in the proper column in the cash record on page 80. Figure the new balance after each item has been recorded. The first three items have been recorded for you.

Line	Date	Explanation	Amount
Line 4	Oct. 15	Cash on hand	$20.75
Line 5	Oct. 15	Salary	$615.52
Line 6	Oct. 16	Rent	$295.00
Line 7	Oct. 16	IRA savings	$20.00
Line 8	Oct. 17	Groceries	$42.86
Line 9	Oct. 18	Gasoline credit card	$39.72
Line 10	Oct. 19	Movie and dinner	$16.00
Line 11	Oct. 20	Dry cleaning	$10.00
Line 12	Oct. 21	Oil and lube	$19.50
Line 13	Oct. 22	Football tickets	$15.00
Line 14	Oct. 24	Groceries	$40.24
Line 15	Oct. 25	Haircut	$10.00
Line 16	Oct. 26	Grooming needs	$6.75
Line 17	Oct. 28	Gasoline	$16.78
Line 18	Oct. 29	Medical expenses	$10.00
Line 19	Oct. 31	Insurance	$50.00
Line 20	Oct. 31	Utility bills	$40.00

CASH RECORD

		A		B	C		D		E	
1		*Victor Won*								
2		*October 15, 1998 to October 31, 1998*								
3		**Date**		**Explanation**	**Cash/Income**		**Expense**		**Balance**	
4		*Oct*	*15*	*Cash on Hand*	*20*	*75*			*20*	*75*
5			*15*	*Salary*	*615*	*52*			*636*	*27*
6			*16*	*Rent*			*295*	*00*	*341*	*27*
7										
8										
9										
10										
11										
12										
13										
14										
15										
16										
17										
18										
19										
20										
21										
22										
23										
24										
25										
26										

Closing Victor's Cash Record

Victor must prove the accuracy of his cash record at the end of his budget period. To do this, he must close his cash record.

■ Help Victor close his cash record on the form on page 80. Follow the steps listed below.

1. Look at line 20 of the cash record form. Add the figures in the cash/income column and in the expense column. These figures are your temporary totals. Write them in pencil below line 20.

2. Prove the accuracy of Victor's temporary totals.

   a. What is Victor's cash on hand on October 15? Look at line 4 of the cash record. _____

   b. What is Victor's salary? _____

   c. What is Victor's total cash/income? _____

   d. What are Victor's total expenses? _____

   e. What is Victor's balance on October 31? _____

3. Does the final balance agree with the balance for the temporary totals in the cash record? If it does not, you must look for the error and correct it.

4. Write the totals in ink. Draw a double-ruled line underneath line 21 to close the cash record for the budget period.

You have now completed Victor Won's budget and cash records for the period of October 15 to October 31.

UNIT 6 *BUDGETS AND CASH RECORDS* 81

Comparing Victor's Budget Plan and Cash Record Lesson 4

Preparing a budget and a cash record helps a person find out whether he or she has lived within the budget. This activity will help you decide whether Victor Won used good money management skills.

■ Answer the following questions about Victor's budget plan and cash record.

1. How much was Victor's estimated income in his budget plan? _____

2. How much was Victor's total income in his cash record? _____

3. What was the difference between Victor's estimated income in his budget and the total income in his cash record? Was one figure higher? _____

   _____

4. How much were Victor's estimated expenses in his budget plan? _____

5. How much were Victor's total expenses in his cash record? _____

6. What was the difference between Victor's estimated expenses in his budget and the total expenses in his cash record? Was one figure higher? _____

   _____

7. Did Victor live within his budget during the budget period? Explain your answer.

   _____

   _____

   _____

   _____

   _____

   _____

   _____

   _____

   _____

   _____

Ann Martin's Budget

Help Ann Martin prepare her budget plan for the pay period of September 1 to September 15. She will have the following income.

Cash on hand—$12.50   Salary—$454.43

Ann also expects the following expenses during this budget period.

Room and Board $100.00	Savings $15.00
Transportation $40.00	Clothing $60.00
Dental Work $70.00	Entertainment $30.00
Vacation Fund $12.00	Medical Expenses $50.00
Lunches $20.00	Insurance $30.00
Miscellaneous $30.00	

A Help Ann prepare her budget plan for the two-week pay period. Use the budget form on page 84.

B Answer the following questions about Ann's budget plan.

1. How much is Ann's estimated income? _____

2. How much are Ann's estimated expenses? _____

3. How much money does Ann expect to have at the end of the budget period?

   _____

Budget Record Form

_____
_____
_____

Cash on Hand:

Estimated Income (Salary/Wages):

TOTAL ESTIMATED CASH:

Estimated Expenses:

TOTAL ESTIMATED EXPENSES $

Total Estimated Cash $ _____

Total Estimated Expenses — _____

CASH ON HAND
(end of Budget Period)

Ann's Cash Record

Ann Martin is keeping a cash record for her two-week budget period. Help Ann record the following items in her cash record.

 Use the form on page 86. Record each item below on the correct line and in the proper column. Figure the new balance after each item has been recorded.

Line	Date	Explanation	Amount
Line 4	Sept. 1	Cash on hand	$ 12.50
Line 5	Sept. 1	Salary	$454.43
Line 6	Sept. 1	Savings	$ 15.00
Line 7	Sept. 2	Room and board	$100.00
Line 8	Sept. 3	Movie and snack	$ 14.60
Line 9	Sept. 7	Bus tickets	$ 20.00
Line 10	Sept. 8	Vacation fund	$ 12.00
Line 11	Sept. 9	Medical expenses	$ 50.00
Line 12	Sept. 10	Bowling	$ 7.00
Line 13	Sept. 11	Grooming needs	$ 9.98
Line 14	Sept. 12	Lunches	$ 20.00
Line 15	Sept. 13	Bus tickets	$ 20.00
Line 16	Sept. 14	Bought a sweater	$ 36.00
Line 17	Sept. 14	Miscellaneous	$ 4.56
Line 18	Sept. 15	Bought a blouse	$29.76
Line 19	Sept. 15	Grooming needs	$ 4.25
Line 20	Sept. 15	Dental work	$70.00
Line 21	Sept. 15	Insurance	$30.00
Line 22	Sept. 15	Bought a CD	$12.95

CASH RECORD

Ann Martin
September 1, 1998—September 15, 1998

	A		B		C	D	E
	Date		Explanation		Cash/Income	Expense	Balance
4							
5							
6							
7							
8							
9							
10							
11							
12							
13							
14							
15							
16							
17							
18							
19							
20							
21							
22							
23							
24							
25							
26							

Closing Ann's Cash Record

Ann must prove the accuracy of her cash record at the end of the budget period. To do this, she must close her cash record.

■ Help Ann close her cash record on the form on page 86. Follow the steps listed below.

1. Look at line 22 of the cash record form. Add the figures in the cash/income column and in the expense column. These figures are your temporary totals. Write them in pencil below line 22.

2. Prove the accuracy of Ann's temporary totals.

   a. What is Ann's cash on hand on September 1? Look at line 4 of the cash record. _____

   b. What is Ann's salary? _____

   c. What is Ann's total cash/income? _____

   d. What are Ann's total expenses? _____

   e. What is Ann's balance on September 15? _____

3. Does the final balance agree with the balance for the temporary totals in the cash record? If it does not, you must look for the error and correct it.

4. Write the totals in ink. Draw a double-ruled line underneath line 23 to close the cash record for the budget period.

You have now completed Ann Martin's budget and cash records for the period of September 1 to September 15.

Ann Is Learning to Save Money

Comparing Ann's Budget Plan and Cash Record   Lesson 8

Preparing a budget and a cash record helps a person find out whether he or she has lived within the budget. This activity will help you decide whether Ann Martin used good money management skills.

■ Answer the following questions about Ann's budget plan and cash record.

1. How much was Ann's estimated income in her budget plan? _____

2. How much was Ann's total income in her cash record? _____

3. What was the difference between Ann's estimated income in her budget and the total income in her cash record? Was one figure higher? _____

   _____

4. How much were Ann's estimated expenses in her budget plan? _____

5. How much were Ann's total expenses in her cash record? _____

6. What was the difference between Ann's estimated expenses in her budget and the total expenses in her cash record? Was one figure higher? _____

   _____

7. Did Ann live within her budget during the budget period? Explain your answer.

   _____

   _____

   _____

   _____

   _____

   _____

   _____

   _____

   _____

   _____

   _____

Your Budget Plan

Now, you are going to prepare a budget for yourself. You have just gotten your first full-time job. This job pays $5.00 per hour. Your net pay each week is $149.12 after deductions. Your cash on hand is $3.25. You are going to share an apartment with two friends. Your share of the rent is $75.00. You will have to decide how much money you will spend on lunches and bus fares. You can also decide how much money you will spend on any other expenses or wants that you can afford out of your total income.

A Use the budget record form on page 90 to prepare your two-week budget. Remember that your expenses cannot be more than your total income.

B Answer the following questions about your budget.

1. How much is your estimated income? _____

2. How much are your estimated expenses? _____

3. How much money do you expect to have at the end of your budget period?

_____

**Can You Include a Mountain
Bike in Your Budget?**

Budget Record Form

Cash on Hand:

Estimated Income (Salary/Wages):

TOTAL ESTIMATED CASH:

Estimated Expenses:

TOTAL ESTIMATED EXPENSES $

Total Estimated Cash $

Total Estimated Expenses —

CASH ON HAND
(end of Budget Period)

Your Cash Record

C Complete the cash record form on page 92. Be sure that you enter all necessary figures and information. Follow the steps listed below.

1. Record each item on the correct line and in the proper column. Figure the balance after each item has been recorded.

2. Close the cash record. Add the figures in the cash/income column and in the expense column. These figures are your temporary totals. Write them in pencil below your last entry.

3. Prove the accuracy of your temporary totals.

   a. What is the cash on hand? Look at line 4 of your cash record.

   _____

   b. What is your salary? _____

   c. What is your total cash/income? _____

   d. What are your total expenses? _____

   e. What is your last balance? _____

4. Does your last balance agree with the balance for the temporary totals? If it does not, you must look for the error and correct it.

5. When your totals are accurate, write them in ink on your form. Add the word *totals*. Draw a double-ruled line underneath these totals.

You have now closed your cash record. You are handling your money well if you have some cash on hand at the end of your budget period.

CASH RECORD

		A	B	C	D	E
1						
2						
3		Date	Explanation	Cash/Income	Expense	Balance
4						
5						
6						
7						
8						
9						
10						
11						
12						
13						
14						
15						
16						
17						
18						
19						
20						
21						
22						
23						
24						
25						
26						

Comparing Your Budget Plan and Cash Record   Lesson 11

Preparing a budget plan and a cash record will help you find out whether you have lived within your budget. This activity will help you decide whether you used good money management skills.

■ You have just completed a budget plan and a cash record for yourself. Write the answers to the following questions about these forms.

1. How much was your estimated income in your budget plan? _____

2. How much was your total income in your cash record? _____

3. What was the difference between your estimated income in your budget and the total income in your cash record? Was one figure higher? _____

   _____

4. How much were your estimated expenses in your budget plan? _____

5. How much were your total expenses in your cash record? _____

6. What was the difference between your estimated expenses in your budget and your total expenses in your cash record? Was one figure higher? _____

   _____

7. Did you live within your budget during the two-week period? Explain your answer.

   _____
   _____
   _____
   _____
   _____
   _____
   _____
   _____
   _____
   _____
   _____

Test Units 5–6

A Unscramble the following words.

1. EDSNE _____

2. DGUBTE _____

3. SCHA NO AHND _____

4. EXFID PSXEESNE _____

5. TWSAN _____

6. LAASRY _____

7. VUELSA _____

8. CABEANL _____

9. NFNIAOTLI _____

10. HCAS RRODEC _____

B Define the following terms.

11. decision making _____

_____

12. temporary totals _____

_____

13. variable expenses _____

_____

14. spending habits _____

_____

15. goals _____

_____

16. gross income _____

_____

17. net income _____

_____

18. explanation column _____

_____

19. balance column _____

_____

20. cash record _____

_____

End-of-Book Test

A Joe Turner has the following needs and wants. Complete each item.

1. Mark each item with an "N" for need or a "W" for want.

   a. _____ rent payment   f. _____ groceries

   b. _____ new car   g. _____ medical bills

   c. _____ new suit   h. _____ credit card payments

   d. _____ entertainment   i. _____ vacation fund

   e. _____ utility bill   j. _____ insurance

2. Write a sentence about Joe's spending habits. _____

   _____

3. List three ways in which Joe could improve his spending habits. _____

   _____

   _____

B Susan Moreno has to manage her money. Use the following information to help her prepare the cash record form on page 96 for the period of September 15 to September 21. Find the current balance after each expense.

Line 4	Sept. 15	$21.85 Cash on Hand
Line 5	Sept. 15	$362.47 Salary
Line 5	Sept. 15	$384.32 New Balance
Line 6	Sept. 15	Susan deposited $30.00 in her savings fund.
Line 7	Sept. 16	Susan spent $15.00 on lunch with a friend.
Line 8	Sept. 17	Susan spent $105.00 on her rent.
Line 9	Sept. 18	Susan spent $40.00 as a down payment on a new sofa.
Line 10	Sept. 19	Susan spent $80.00 making payments on two of her credit cards.
Line 11	Sept. 20	Susan deposited $20.00 into her vacation fund.
Line 12	Sept. 21	Susan spent $60.00 on a health club membership.

4. What is Susan's income? _____

5. What is her total cash/income? _____

6. What are her total expenses? _____

7. What is her final balance? _____

CASH RECORD

	A		B	C	D	E
3	Date		Explanation	Cash/Income	Expense	Balance
4						
5						
6						
7						
8						
9						
10						
11						
12						
13						
14						
15						
16						
17						
18						
19						
20						
21						
22						
23						
24						
25						
26						